Contents

iv

Shadow Rap

There's a shadow with no name
that is waiting down the street,
with its dirty fingernails
and big boots on its feet.

I'm afraid to meet its glare
but I dare not look away.
I pretend that I don't care
but it steps into my day.

It holds out greedy hands
and stares me in the eyes.
I grip my pockets tightly
and hope that shadow dies.

I slow my pace right down,
but I know we have to meet . . .
for that shadow with no name
waits for *me* down the street.

Voices in my Head

I daren't!

You can do it.

I can't!

You can do it.

What if . . . ?

You can do it.

Perhaps . . .

You can do it.

DARE I do it?

You can do it.

Well, MAYBE I should . . .

You can do it.

I DID IT!

I said you could do it.

I knew I would!

The Gary Gunter Rap
(or, He Loves Me, He Loves Me Not!)

There's a guy called Gary Gunter
and he says that he loves Dee.
He says that he loves Dee
but she's chasing Johnny Lea!

There's a guy called Johnny Lea
and he's chased by that girl Dee.
He says he doesn't want her
and he says that he loves *me*!

There's a guy called Gary Gunter
and I don't think he's so clever
as he *still* says he loves Dee
though she says she'll love him never!

There's a guy called Johnny Lea
who was chased by that girl Dee.
Now *she* wants Gary Gunter
but Gary's after ME!

Have you Read . . .?

Enjoy your homework	by R.U. Joking
Out for the count	by I.C. Stars
Cliff-top rescue	by Justin Time
A year in space	by Esau Mars
Your turn to wash up	by Y. Mee
Off to the dentist	by U. First
Broken windows	by E. Dunnit
Pickpocket Pete	by M.T. Purse
Lions on the loose	by Luke Out
Helping Gran	by B.A. Dear
Ten ice-creams	by Segovia Flaw
Rock concert	by Q. Here

Harvest Hymn

We plough the fields and scatter
our pesticides again.
Our seeds are fed and watered
by gentle acid rain.
We spray the corn in winter
till pests and weeds are dead –
who minds a little poison
inside his daily bread?

All good gifts around us
beneath our ozone layer
are safe, oh Lord,
so thank you Lord
that we know how to care.

Something to Do in a Traffic Jam

Dream of
a world where bat
and tiger wander free
and turtles set their courses by
the stars.

Progress Man

Hurry now! *cried Progress,*
and just see what I can do!
Watch my chainsaw, feel my axe.
My ways are great for you,

'cos I'm a swinging, singing,
racing, chasing, do-it-how-I-can,
I am the swinging, singing,
racing, chasing Progress Man!

See me chop your forests down,
we need a motorway!
You have some roads already . . .?
Well, not enough, I say,

and I'm a swinging, singing
racing, chasing, do-it-how-I-can,
I am the swinging, singing,
racing, chasing Progress Man!

What's a little drop of oil
spilt over golden sand?
It's just a tiny price to pay,
the world has so much land,

and I'm a swinging, singing,
racing, chasing, do-it-how-I-can,
I am the swinging, singing,
racing, chasing Progress Man!

Riddle

For want of a word
the thought was lost.
For want of a thought
the tree was lost.
For want of a tree
the forest was lost.
For want of the forest
a land was lost.
For want of a land
the people were lost,
and all for the want
of one small word . . .

. . . why?

Sealsong

Around me, seas
stretch endlessly,
above me, sky.
A space to breathe,
a place to swim,
to pace the days
by moon or sun.
A place that time
had kept from man,

no place to die.

Two-week Holiday Diary of Man of Few Words

13 August	**England**.
14 August	**Rain again.**
15 August	**Plane.**
16 August	**Spain.**
17 August	**Sun.**
18 August	**Fun.**
19 August	**Sea.**
20 August	**Sand.**
21 August	**Sea.**
22 August	**Fun.**
23 August	**Sun.**
24 August	**Spain.**
25 August	**Plane again.**
26 August	**Rain.**
27 August	**England.**

Eight Things to Do on a Beach

Stretch out on hot sand,
wriggle fingers warmed by the sun.

Catch a wave in a bucket.
Circle your castle with a hundred shells,
then choose your favourite one.

Smell the sea-salt air,
taste breeze-blown sand in picnic bread.
Remember the cry of seagulls
when day is done.

Taddy Tale

There once was a tadpole called Fred,
who lived in a wet, weedy bed.
He hated the view
so grew legs two by two . . .
Now Fred is a fat frog instead!

Explosive Tale

There was a volcano called Dot –
once on maps just a minuscule spot.
But, 'I'm hungry!' Dot grumbled
as her insides rumbled.
'And, what's more, I'm feeling quite hot!'

The Romans in Britain
(A History in 40 Words)

The Romans gave us aqueducts,
fine buildings and straight roads,
where all those Roman legionaries
marched with heavy loads.

They gave us central heating,
good laws, a peaceful home . . .
then after just four centuries
they shuffled back to Rome.

Remembrance Day
11th November

Poppies? Oh, miss,
can I take round the tray?
It's only history next.
We're into '45 –
I *know* who won the war,
no need to stay.

> *Old man wears his flower*
> *with pride, his numbers dying now –*
> *but that's no news.*

Why buy? –
Because I'm asked
because a flower looks good
to match my mate
not to seem too mean . . .
(what's ten pence anyway
to those of us who grew
with oranges, December lettuce
and square fish?)

Yes, I'll wear it –
for a while.
Until it's lost
or maybe picked apart
during some boring television news
and then, some idle moment,
tossed.

> Poppies? Who cares
> as long as there's
> some corner of a foreign field
> to bring me pineapple, papaya
> and my two weeks' patch of sun? –
> But I'll still have one
> if you really want.
> It isn't quite my scene, but then –
> at least the colour's fun.

Old man stumbles
through November mud,
still keeps his silence
at the eleventh hour.

Anne Boleyn

Would you like to be a queen
with a crown upon your head?
Would you join the king in court,
and share the royal bed?

Would you like to be a queen,
to spread your wit and charm,
with a crown upon your head . . .
and your head beneath your arm?

Make Your Own Monster:
A DIY Guide

How do you make a monster?

Not with the glare of a torch-eye
slicing into the dark.
Not with a gash of yellow paint
or the swing of a bat-wing cloak.
Nor with the roar of a dinosaur
or a sudden ruler-crack,
nor with egg boxes, staples, glue . . .

This is what you do . . .

You lie awake after twilight
under a starless sky.
You leave your window just ajar
and feel the night creep by.
When the window squeaks
you start to sweat,
you remember the wind is still
and yet . . .

A creak in the hall
crawls on to the stair
and you know that somehow,
something is there . . .

Your mouth is dry
and the hairs on your back
stand to attention,
stopped in their track.
And a shadow crouches
by the door . . .
gathers breath
then slowly creeps

across the floor

TOWARDS YOU!

Then, you can be sure,
you've made your monster!

Who's Afraid?

Fear disappears in the daytime
when you say goodbye to night,
for the shadows that lingered in darkness
all vanish before the light.

No one's afraid in the morning
when dark dreams fade from sight,
but if fear prowls back to haunt you
it prowls back in the black of night.